they will always find their way back to you, regardless.

Ace Tiwari

they will always find their way back to you, regardless.

Presentation by *BookLeaf Publishing*

Web: www.bookleafpub.com

E-mail: info@bookleafpub.com

ISBN: 978-93-95890-46-5

First edition 2022

DEDICATION

Dedicated to the hopeless romantics who have never fallen in love (yet). Listen to some Taylor Swift songs, they might help fill the void in your heart <3. Conan Gray songs are good for when one is heartbroken and/or depressed </3.

PREFACE

I'm young, so I don't know much about love. I've only gathered knowledge from books, movies, music, and observing other people experiencing love. I've concluded that love can be expressed in many ways, and it isn't always about romance. Platonic love is equally as important, as is familial love. Love isn't restricted, and it can be perceived so differently. Hatred is a type of love. Love is so many things, not least complex. I don't pretend to "be in love" (ew, not for me) or to understand love, but I respect it. This book is a collection of poetry about me interpreting love, drawing inspiration from books and music.

appreciation of the mundane.

society believes that beauty is extra, that beauty is privilege.

but I believe beauty is also simplicity.

the beauty of nature in the simplicity of trees and plants swaying with the wind.
the solace of reliance when the stars shine every night without fail.
the beauty of animals helping each other, protecting their families.
the beauty of mundane differences.
the beauty of simple yet unique traits in people, places, things.
the beauty in knowing humanity is so alike each other, while simultaneously being so different.
the relief of accepting the unknown.

simple things that are so beautiful.

noted.

he adores music and plays piano. he, unlike most teenage boys, actually enjoys the company of his younger siblings. he makes a constant effort to check in with everyone, generously offering a shoulder to cry on. he goes out of his way to perform random acts of kindness, always offering a friendly smile. he has an indifferent relationship with mathematics and despises science. in the evenings, he always waters the garden, using the time to bond with his mother. he twists his hands in his lap when he's nervous, he walks a little higher when he's joyous. he has always made his hair a specific style to be more like his father. he makes little handmade presents and spontaneously gifts them to those closest to him, friends and family. he enjoys literature and reads in secret. often, he catches himself smiling as he reads, realising how much the ink on the pages mean to him. he cherishes the smell of new books, delicately turning each page. he worships healthy love found in fiction, yearning for a cliche love story. yearning for someone to perceive him not just by his looks, but by his personality and behaviour, too.

his friend beside him noticed all this. he noticed the way all these little quirks were performed so subtlety and instinctively. he smiled, knowing he was the one who noticed him for all his is. he wondered when the other was ever going to realise, all he ever wanted, ever needed, was right in front of him.

stolen glances.

a joke is told,
laughs sound around the room,
your eyes find hers.

her eyes shine with humor, which you could feel reflected in yours.
you share a smile, quietly giddy with the knowledge of something no one else in the room holds.

the knowledge of the way she organises her kitchen utensils, her closet. the way her shoulders scrunch up when she laughs, the way she's prone to forgetting the simplest things. the way she always has a book in her bag, the way she has a playlist for every situation imaginable. the way she looks when she sleeps, the way she's somehow still so effortlessly ethereal when she wakes up. the way she's genuinely kind to every soul she comes across, the way her heart is so pure.

the way you know her eyes will always find yours in a crowded room.

the knowledge that you hold her heart, as she holds yours.

polaroid pictures.

walks along the beach,
sunset picnics,
polaroid clicks.

legs dangling over the skate rink,
you take her flannel,
polaroid clicks.

sitting in a park bench,
pages are turned in unison,
polaroid clicks.

the laptop screen blares "10 Things I Hate About You",
rants about Kat are exchanged,
polaroid clicks.

she strums the guitar,
you press the keys of the piano,
a smile is shared.

polaroid clicks.

fruitless wishing.

all she wanted was for him to turn around, to apologise, to promise to be better, and uphold that promise. she wanted him to come running after her, knocking on her door at 2am with a bouquet of roses and a tear-stained face.

she knew it was high unlikely he was going turn back, but still. she could see it play out in her mind so clearly...

her phone buzzed.

she sat up and unlocked it. it was a text from him, apologising for what he's done, promising to be a better man, telling her he loves her.
it was a text from him, that had everything she wanted.

her heart glowed and her eyes watered. maybe she was wrong, and him acting like a jerk was just some weird phase.

a sneeze scared her awake.

or maybe she was right all along.

she groaned, realising it was just a daydream, a fantasy. she was disappointed at the lack of notifications her phone held. he truly wasn't going to change.

this epiphany led her to unlock her phone, delete their conversations and block his number. he wasn't going to change, but she was. she was going to change for herself, look forward and never think of him again. she deserved way better and dwelling on the past was not going to help her.

she went to the store and bought a pack of hair dye.

inseparable, they were.

he was her first love, and only later would she
realise, her first miscalculation.
her earliest experience of treachery.

15
young and carefree.

she never believed in love at first sight,
but then she met him.

him,
with his laidback and confident demeanour,
cheeky smirk,
reassuring smile,
meaningful hugs.

yet wary of each other, they clicked instantly.
sparks flew, and they kept meeting in secret, for
a family rivalry kept them apart.
inseparable, they were, not unlike a silhouette
following a body.

she was falling, plummeting in love.
she had unknowingly dived so deep; it was
strenuous to pull back.

so, she succumbed, bathing in the blissful
feeling of being in love.

then he did something that abruptly shook her
back to reality.
he did something that made her withdraw so
fast,
she wondered if it was ever real.

she retaliated, breaking both of their hearts even
more.
communication was cut, and she moved away.

18
guarded, apprehensive.

one might say dire circumstances brought them
back together, another might say fate.
regardless, they reunited.

they worked together, and truths were
uncovered,
realisations were made.
they began to hope.

he confessed, then did she.
slowly, they mended the other's fractured heart.
gently, tenderly, delicately, lovingly,
mended the other's shattered heart.

21
living for the other.

all that mattered was each other.

she had never known someone more
kind-hearted than him,
he had never known someone stronger than her.

inseparable, they were,
not unlike the moon and the stars.

he was her first betrayal, but later would she
realise, her true love.

academic rivals to lovers.

the teacher finished asking a question.
two hands shot in the air.
everyone knew from the sound of air rushing
alone, who the hands belonged to.
for these two students had made their rivalry
clear,
the competition tense, the supposed dislike
obvious.
but everyone asked one another, why?

she worked hard to meet her parents'
expectations,
to get into a good university,
to make sure her life has a purpose.
she engaged in this fruitless rivalry because it
added an element of fun in her deary
motivations.

he took his studies intensely for the same
reasons, more or less.
but he sparked the rivalry for her.

beginning to end.

a shy "hi",
feeble introductions.
exchanging phone numbers,
with promises of a coffee date.

a walk to the cinema,
hands tentatively touch, tentatively hold.
a long debate about who's to pay,
arm-in-arm walks in the moonlight.

two knocks on the door,
a bouquet of flowers in one hand, a gift basket in the other.
an excited squeal,
an affectionate hug.

hand in hand,
staring lovingly into each other's eyes.
the priest commences the ceremony,
the best night of their lives.

words whispered in the blanket of the night,
"I love you."
"you are mine, as I am yours."

"I'm with you, from the beginning to the end."

a change of heart.

she hated February.
she disliked the month of love so intensely you'd wonder who hurt her.
all the valentine proposals, roses and chocolates, and cheesy love songs made her want to vomit.
one year, she did.

seeing the perfect couples online,
seeing people happily in love,
without a problem in the world,
it angered her to know that she would never be able to experience that.

or so she believed.

he observed in amusement her dislike for love.
he was positive that one day, she would experience someone loving her so tenderly that she would be forced to have a change of heart.
he was positive she would experience the comfort of being loved and fall in love herself.
he was positive she would have an enlightening, eye-opening, worthwhile journey with love,
and realise that her problem with love wasn't that she hated it,

it was that she hated it because she truly
believed she won't ever experience it.
she truly believed no one will love her.

he wanted her to realise how incorrect that was.
he wanted her to realise that he loved her,
he wanted to be the person who shows her the
magic that love is.

she is now fond of February.

waiting.

he observed in tiresome as another guy asked
her out.
he watched in crippling discomfort as they
embarked on another date.
he looked on in agony as they danced, as they
kissed.
he listened in wearisome as she ranted about
how great her current boyfriend is.

he wondered in impatience if she was ever going
to realise that it should be him,
it has always been him all along.

it was always him who listened to her rant about
her favourite books, favourite movies, favourite
songs.
it was always him who engaged in conversation
with her, never being dry.
it was always him she ran crying to; it was
always him who comforted her.
it has always been him who knew her favourite
things, knew her habits, knew her personality,
knew that she yearns for a romance found in
books.

it has always been him who knew he could give that to her.

autumn evenings.

two girls sat perched in a tree.
a small breeze rippled through it,
the wind gently carrying the autumn leaves,
delicately settling them scattered along the
pavement.

one girl watches the sunset.
watches the vibrant hues of purples, pinks,
oranges,
blend together to paint a mesmerising picture.
watches the way the clouds drift along so
elegantly,
the way bird silhouettes pass through it
purposefully.

the other watches her.
watches the small smile playing on her lips,
the sheer awe in her eyes.
watches the wondrous way the wind so perfectly
blows in her face,
keeping her hair back and emphasising her eyes,
her nose, her mouth.
watches her relaxed posture,
the serenity in her face.

peace blankets over them comfortably.
not suffocating,
freeing.

the girl sighed contentedly.
"it's beautiful, isn't it?"

"yeah", the other girl murmured,

"it is."

her.

the movie blared on the TV screen.
her best friend was engrossed in the movie,
utterly engaged,
while she was captivated by her.

her.
with her kind smile, warm eyes.
her infectious laughter and genuine
compliments.
her,
with her generous soul and humorous mind.
her,
possibly the most beautiful person she has ever
seen,
natural beauty emphasised always.

"what is it? you're staring." her friend questions,
puzzled, snapping her out of her reverie.

"oh... nothing. I'm just going to go... get some
water."
she hurries out of the room, cheeks flaming.

stay gold.

sunsets in general are beautiful,
stunning, ethereal, calming.
like most people, he enjoyed watching the sun
set over the horizon,
hues of reds, oranges, pinks, purples, and blues
blending together to make something truly
enchanting.
he loved the way nature was able to do this,
he simply adored everything about sunsets.

but there was something,
someone,
that made sunsets even more meaningful.
every day, at dusk, he would always set out to
his grave,
bringing his copy of "Gone with the Wind" with
him.
every day, at dusk, he would always set out to
his grave,
and watch the sun set with him.

sorrow.

it wasn't the fact that he was gone which hurt.

it was the fact that he lost him, which hurt.

it was the fact that he will never see his beautiful
dark eyes again,
see the hurt hidden in them, the lost puppy look
covering it.
he will never be able to laugh at his short height,
never be able to ruffle his jet-black hair again.

it was the fact that he deserved such a long,
happy, life,
after everything he had been through at the
young age of 16.
it was the fact that he was his best friend,
soulmate through and through.

it was the fact that he was gone,
and he could have saved him,
that hurt the most.

destined to be together, only to fall apart.

she loved him, really,
but she couldn't be with him,
stay with him.

they were destined to be together,
only to fall apart.
again and again,
heartbreak after heartbreak.

he needed her,
it was true.
he had always loved her and always will,
he knew that.

but he also knew that this repetitive cycle of
wanting each other,
having each other,
breaking each other,
was proving to be too much to handle.
it was taking a mental toll on the both of them,
further injuring their relationship.

but one thing that would remain
forever unharmed

was their love for the other.

they were destined to be together,
only to fall apart,
then mend hand in hand.

new years day.

the party ended a while after the fireworks.
empty bottles and cans lay on the
glitter-covered floor.

a girl sat in a park under the fading moonlight.
this girl was a dreamer, a
romantic. she longed for a flawless fairy-tale.
though young, she knew much
of the world, knew how significant love is. it did
not matter whether the love
was family, platonic, or romantic.

this girl was not necessarily neglected of love,
but she had been deprived of
attention. she yearned for a love – someone,
anyone, who would bring the
light to her darkest days, who would avidly talk
to her, listen to her.

as the girl looked forwards, she saw an
apartment block. peering through the
trees, she noticed only one apartment was still
awake. it had the distinct air of
a finished party, and a couple was cleaning into
the new year.

the two lovers had music playing in the
background, and they danced. eyes
for only each other, they swayed to the music.
the way they looked at each
other – it was indescribable. a look of utter love,
sheer fondness. magical.
that is what it was – magical. the pair were
entranced by each other. it was
clear they could have stayed in that moment
forever.

they resumed cleaning, and the girl watching
could tell they were still
enchanted.

the way he caught her when she slipped and fell,
the way she laughed at his
fruitless attempts at cleaning wine stains. the
way they stayed up to clean the
confetti, collect the polaroids, the way they did it
for each other.

all they needed was each other.

the girl watched on and prayed that one day she
would find a love as pure as theirs.

you're glowing.

an incandescent glow shined from her face.
incredible auburn hair tied back,
posture fixed,
eyes ahead.
she was completely, effortlessly ethereal,
her rich red hair positively radiating.

I blinked, coming to my senses.
realising muscle memory guided my legs the route home,
realising the girl that had walked past me
completely consumed my mind.
for a moment, at least.
I laughed at myself,
the behaviour pathetic,
but predictable and common.

it's nice to have a friend.

she plopped onto a vacant seat at the counter.
she was in an exhilarated mood, ready to see the light in the most unilluminated of places.
ready to not feel enviously bitter at the wholesome couple who sat by the window,
instead appreciate their love,
and hope that one day she'll be as hopelessly in love as them.
she was feeling hopeful, optimistic,
excited to see what new challenges the world will throw at her.

he noticed all this.
he noticed her elated mood from the bounce in her step,
the fix in her posture.
the way she looked around assuredly, instead of shying away from everyone.
he noticed her genuine smile at the waitress, the couple.
he observed how she took her time eating her food, devouring the almond croissant, savouring the hot chocolate.
he noticed she radiated a heartening energy.

he noticed she looked lovely as ever.